INTRODUCTION TO THE BREED

From the "Forbidden City" hidden up on the "Roof of the World," the hermit-theocracy of Tibet, comes that quaint, debonair, self-assertive member of the dog kingdom, the Lhasa Apso.

This is a breed that has been badly misunderstood from the time it was first introduced to the Western World. Early writers, in their manuscripts about Oriental dogs, could not agree on either nomenclature or classification of the Tibetan dogs. The only thing they did agree upon was that there were several distinct types, each with heavy profuse coats, and tails curled up over their backs. By the mid-20th century, the experts finally agreed that the Apso is not a terrier and that it is distinct and different from its cousins the Shih Tzu and the Tibetan Terrier.

The dignified goatee and mustache of the Lhasa Apso combined with its handsome eyefall, parted in the middle and combed to each side, give the breed a resemblance to an Oriental monk or lama.

DESCRIPTION

The sturdy little Apso's most distinctive physical feature is perhaps his long profuse coat. The dog is covered with a coat that is similar to human hair in consistency, and which hangs straight to the ground without wave or curl. In fact, at first glance, one might see only a mop of hair. Underneath it all is an adorable, friendly and utterly delightful animal. To know a Lhasa Apso is to fall completely in love with one. This dear little dog fairly radiates with charm from the tip of his tail, which is carried well over his back, to the end of his nose.

The Tibetans place great importance on coat and color. They will hardly acknowledge a dog with a scanty coat, and of course, the Apso being the "*Tibetan Lion-Dog*," the lion-like colors are greatly prized.

Every Lhasa Apso should have thick hair between his toes. The need for this is obvious, as is the need for the heavy coat, given that Tibet is a country of great contrasts in temperature. The dogs must be able to survive in altitudes of over 15,000 feet, and in tremendous extremes of cold, heat, rain and dryness. The dense coat keeps the dog both warm in the cold and snow and insulates prize dark tips to the ears, beard, and tail.

The coat on the head falls forward covering the eyes; however, many Apso owners prefer to hold the eyefall up with elastic bands or barrettes, so they can see the lovely expression in the eyes of their pets. The beautiful oval dark brown eyes

The Lhasa Apso is covered with a coat that is similar to human hair in consistency, hanging straight to the ground without wave or curl.

him against the heat. The eyefall protects his eyes against the glare of the sun on the snow and the blowing dust. The thick hair between the Lhasa Apso's toes protects the feet.

Besides the goldens, the Apso comes in a variety of colors: sandy, honey, dark grizzle, slate, smoke, black, white, solids, or parti-colors. The Tibetans highly are like the human eye in shape. A topknot is also a sign of the nobility in Tibet.

Another distinctive feature of this handsome breed is the dignified goatee and mustache. This, combined with the handsome eyefall, parted in the middle and combed to each side, gives the Apso a resemblance to an Oriental monk or lama.

The Lhasa Apso is an ideal house dog. The breed thrives on close association with his family members—human or feline.

Although essentially a house dog, the Lhasa loves to spend time outdoors.

TEMPERAMENT

In a country such as Tibet, where dangers may lurk from within as well as from without, the little Apso earns his place in the Tibetan household and in the monasteries as a watchdog. He is called *Abso Seng Kye,* or *Bark, Sentinel Lion Dog.* His function is to sleep near his master and sound a warning should any danger threaten. This is a task for which the Apso is well suited. He has a very keen sense of hearing, is intelligent, and is capable of readily distinguishing between friend and foe. And yet, unlike other small breeds, the Apso is not a nervous or continuous barker. He is more apt to "woof" or growl his warning in a calm and well-mannered way. This particular trait makes the Lhasa Apso a very adaptable pet for city living.

Despite the small size (12 to 16 pounds for bitches, 14 to 18 pounds for males) the Apso is extremely rugged. There is nothing fragile or delicate about the breed. They exude good health and boundless energy but are quick to perceive their master's mood and adapt their own behavior to the mood of the moment. They love a good outdoor romp but are essentially house dogs.

The Apso has a happy, gay, almost jaunty gait. The front legs are extended directly forward as they walk, with the rear feet extending directly to the rear, so the pads of the rear feet are seen peeking out from under the coat as the dog walks. The overall appearance is one of symmetry and good form, as the Apso is well put together, compact and extremely regal and aristocratic in bearing. And yet, in spite of this aloof demeanor, there is something of the clown apparent in this delightful animal.

ENVIRONMENT

The Apso is a hardy breed—it can survive happily just about anywhere. Colonel Duncan's Tomu was taken directly from Tibet to Kathmandu, then immediately to Jodhpur, one of the hottest places in India. And, after living in Jodhpur a number of years, he was taken to England, surviving all temperature changes without a bit of difficulty. The Apso's adaptability to change is one of its most unequaled

characteristics. They are a long-lived breed, not fully maturing until about three years of age. On July 4, 1964, Ch. Hamilton La Pung, owned by Mrs. Elizabeth Finn, of Cedar Grove, New Jersey, passed away at the ripe old age of 29. This almost unbelievable little white Apso would have been 30 in November of 1964, and that would be equivalent to more than a century and half in human terms.

Lhasa Apsos thrive on affection and close association with humans. They are not a breed that can be banished to the garage or basement. Long years of close human association has made them ideal house dogs. Yet they are always ready for a romp outdoors or car ride with their humans.

One of the most appealing attributes of the Lhasa Apso is the wide variety of coat colors. Here are a pair of parti-colored pups and a golden adult.

LHASA APSO STANDARD

A breed standard is the criterion by which the appearance (and to a certain extent, the temperament as well) of any given dog is made subject to objective measurement. Basically, the standard for any breed is a definition of the perfect dog to developments in a breed by checking the publications of your national kennel club. Printed below is the American Kennel Club standard for the Lhasa Apso.

Character—Gay and assertive, but chary of strangers.

The beautiful oval dark brown eyes of the Lhasa Apso are like the human eye in shape.

which all specimens of the breed are compared. Breed standards are always subject to change through review by the national breed club for each dog, so that it is always wise to keep up with

Size—Variable, but about 10 inches or 11 inches at shoulder for dogs, bitches slightly smaller.

Color—All colors equally acceptable with or without dark tips to ears and beard.

The veil or fall is the portion of a Lhasa Apso's head furnishings that hangs straight down over the eyes and at least partially covers them. Drawing by John Quinn.

Body Shape—The length from point of shoulders to point of buttocks longer than height at withers, well ribbed up, strong loin, well-developed quarters and thighs.

Coat—Heavy, straight, hard, not woolly nor silky, of good length, and very dense.

Mouth and Muzzle—The preferred bite is either level or slightly undershot. Muzzle of medium length: a square muzzle is objectionable.

Head—Heavy head furnishings with good fall over eyes, good whiskers and beard: skull narrow, falling away behind the eyes in a marked degree, not quite flat, but not domed or apple-shaped: straight foreface of fair length. Nose black, the length from tip of nose to eye to be roughly about one-third of the total length from nose to back of skull.

Eyes—Dark brown, neither very large and full, nor very small and sunk.

Ears—Pendant, heavily feathered.

Legs—Forelegs straight: both forelegs and hind legs heavily furnished with hair.

Feet—Well feathered, should be round and catlike, with good pads.

Tail and Carriage—Well feathered, should be carried well over back in a screw: there may be a kink at the end. A low carriage of stern is a serious fault.

The Lhasa Apso's most distinct feature is his long profuse coat. The dense coat keeps him warm in the cold and insulates him in the heat.

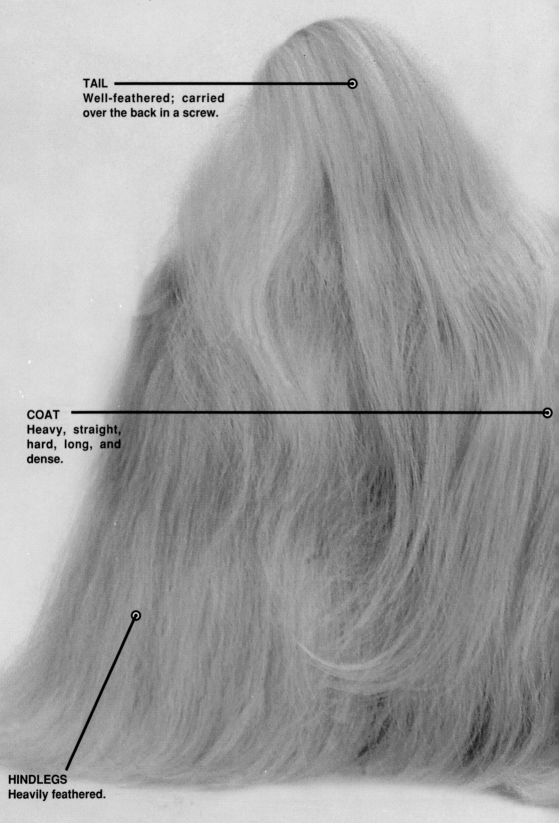

1995 Westminster Best of Breed Winner Ch. Hoshira Hylan Shotru Brie owned by Michael A. Santora and Alan J. Loso.

TAIL
Well-feathered; carried over the back in a screw.

COAT
Heavy, straight, hard, long, and dense.

HINDLEGS
Heavily feathered.

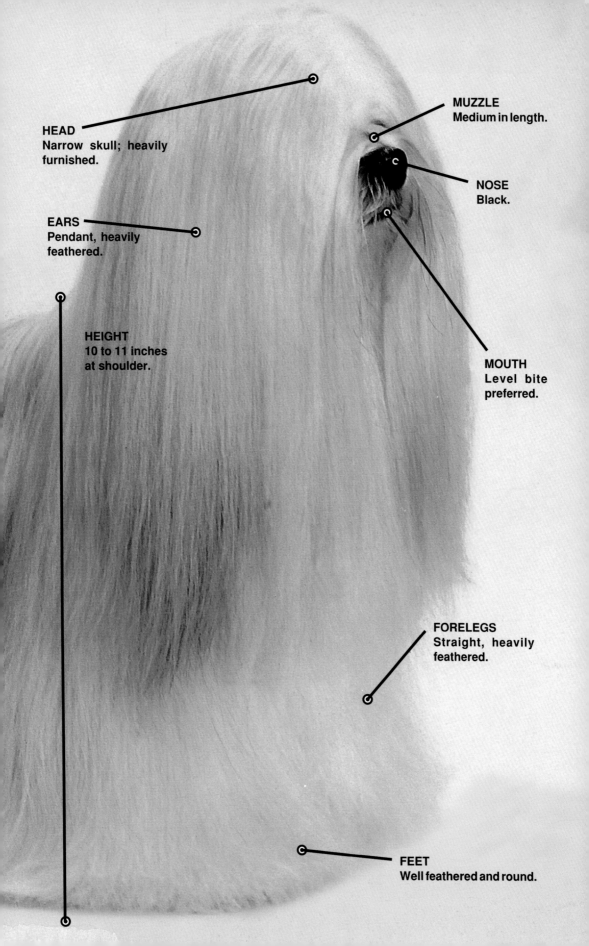

HEAD
Narrow skull; heavily
furnished.

MUZZLE
Medium in length.

NOSE
Black.

EARS
Pendant, heavily
feathered.

HEIGHT
10 to 11 inches
at shoulder.

MOUTH
Level bite
preferred.

FORELEGS
Straight, heavily
feathered.

FEET
Well feathered and round.

HISTORY OF THE BREED

Recorded history of the Lhasa Apso goes as far back as 800 BC. Since then the breed has thrived in the *Potala* (the Dalai Lama's palace and monastery), other monasteries in or near Lhasa, and in the homes of Tibetan nobles. It is impossible to buy one of the dogs in Tibet, for they are never sold. From the beginning of the Manchu Dynasty in 1583 and as recently as 1908, it was the practice of the Dalai Lama to send Apsos as sacred gifts with his blessing to the Manchu Emperors of China and members of the Imperial families. The Apsos, which were always sent in pairs, were supposed to be bringers of good luck and prosperity, and it was a great honor to receive a pair. Mr. Mukandi Lalk writing for the Indian Kennel Club *Gazette*, tells us that these "strange little long haired small dogs" were at one time called Talisman dogs and *Sheng Trou*. Sheng, of course, is related to the Tibetan word for lion. Some art historians today say that the carvings of lions in Oriental art are modeled on the Apso.

It is believed that the word "apso" is a corruption of the Tibetan word "rapso" which means goatlike, likening the Apso to the small longhaired Tibetan goat.

"Satru" and "Sona," two exceptionally fine golden Apsos, were bred by two early famous breeders, Mrs. F. M. Bailey and Mrs. A.C. Dudley. In 1934 both these dogs won firsts in Open classes, and both were judged Best of Breed.

Mr. Rahul Sandrityayan, an Indian scholar of the Tibetan language, tells us that Apso means "wholely covered with hair all over," and that the Apso has come to mean a small dog covered with hair all over. It is also believed that the word "apso" is a corruption of the Tibetan word "rapso" which means goatlike, likening the Apso to the small, longhaired Tibetan goat.

There are certain villages around Lhasa where the Apsos are bred. The lamas and rich Tibetans search for them and obtain all that are available. They do not use them merely as pets. In the monasteries and the houses of the nobility they are used as sentinels inside the house. Their breeding for generations as watchdogs have made the Lhasas unusually keen and intelligent. They are affectionate and devoted pets.

How, or why, the Lhasa Apso came to be called the Lion Dog of Tibet is really not definitely known. In fact, it is not definitely known why the sacred emblem of the Lion plays such an important part in Tibetan art and lore. Obviously there are no lions in Tibet now, and recorded history gives us no indications that there ever were any lions in Tibet. And yet, "Sengtri, the Lion Throne" of the Dalai Lama, was built in accordance with instructions in ancient Tibetan scriptures. It is square and made of gilded wood supported by eight lions, two at each corner. The Tibetan flag is composed of two green lions with a yellow sun and snow-capped mountain superimposed on a background of blue and red rays. The relationship of the Lion Dog danger. Statues and objects of art picture this small dog with a heavy mane of hair around its neck and a tail proudly up-curled over its back with the Manjuri Buddha's pet dog. It doesn't take much imagination to identify the Lhasa. It especially isn't hard to imagine if you are a Tibetan and strongly believe in reincarnation. The identification of

Lhasas were a little known breed in England in the early 1930s. These examples, gathered for a Cheltenham Show in 1933, are among the first genuine dogs imported to Britain.

to a true lion is obviously symbolic. One connotation might be in the person of the Manjuri Buddha, the God of Learning, who is sometimes pictured with a small pet dog beside him. Buddhist theology tells us that this small pet could be transformed into a lion should the need arise, and could then be used by the Manjuri Buddha to escape the Lhasa Apso with the lion could well be furthered because of the little animal's habit when confronted by danger or an unwelcome intruder of pawing the ground, assuming a sturdy stance, and in all respects looking like a small lion. Again, this identification is reflected by the Tibetans when they affectionately

This dog is said to be a Chinese Lion Dog. The relationship of the Lion Dog to a true lion is obviously symbolic.

call their dogs *Abso Seng Kye*, or *Bark, Sentinel Lion Dog.*

All purebred Lhasas in existence outside the city of Lhasa in Tibet stem from pairs that were given as gifts to high officials, people of importance visiting the country, and the courts of China.

THE LHASA APSO IN ENGLAND

Among the non-Tibetans who have received Apsos as gifts is Mr. Henrich Harrer, who was unable to care for his dog during long marches across the Chang Tang Plateau, and was forced to leave him with nomads. American writer and newsman, Lowell Thomas, Jr., pictured a pair of Apsos in his book *Out of This World.* Mrs. Margaret Hayes, who wrote about the breeds of Tibet in 1933, owned several of the dogs. Colonel R.C. Duncan of the British Army received his Tomu of Tibet from a lama he met at Kathmandu, the capital of Nepal. The lama had come to Kathmandu directly from Lhasa on a pilgrimage and brought his young pet along. The Colonel and lama carried on a correspondence for a number of years and the lama never failed to inquire about the health and happiness of "his Tomu." Colonel Duncan brought Tomu to England in 1947 when he retired from the British Army. He kept her in her original Tibetan garb—unwashed, unbrushed, and hair plaited and twisted. But Tomu was not the first Lhasa in England; these shaggy, short-legged little dogs

were introduced in 1904, brought in by members of the Younghusband expedition to Tibet. The breed did not really make headway in England until Lieutenant-Colonel F.M. Bailey, British Minister in Nepal, and Mrs. Bailey returned to England in the late 1930s. Mrs. Bailey was responsible for correcting the English nomenclature, as prior to their return, the dogs were known as "Lhasa Terriers." After the Baileys returned to England the dogs were correctly called Lhasa Apsos. Mrs. Bailey started her kennel from a pair of dogs given to her by Lieutenant Colonel R.S. Kennedy who, while on a mission to Lhasa with Sir Charles Bell in 1921, was given the dogs as a present from Tsarong Shape, who was the Commander-in-Chief of the Tibetan Army at that time. Colonel Bailey succeeded in obtaining some more Apsos when he was in Lhasa in 1924.

The first Lhasas (called Lhasa Terriers or Tibetan Terriers interchangeably at that time) brought into England after the Younghusband expedition were mostly blue-black and white, or all black, or grizzle in color and were generally larger and coarser than the smaller variety of golden Apsos brought in by the Baileys. In the early 1930s, Lady Browning brought some small dogs into England which she had acquired in China. She called her dogs Tibetan Lion Dogs. These dogs were admitted to the Lhasa Apso Club and the club name was changed to The

Apso and Lion Dog Club. In 1933 the first class for Apsos was held at W.E.L.K.S. Championship show, and all three varieties were shown under the classification of "Tibetan Breeds." These dogs, at that time, were referred to as though they were one and the same breed, a situation which no doubt was the basis for considerable confusion and controversy about the Tibetan breeds. In fact, the first Tibetan breed champion, Ch. Rupso, whose stuffed body now occupies a place of honor in the Natural History Museum in South Kensington, was referred to as a Lhasa Terrier, Tibetan Terrier, and Lhasa Apso. Then in England there was another name change, the English referred to the breed as the Tibetan Apso. Eventually, the "varieties" of the Tibetan breeds in England were separated into what is now known as the Tibetan Terrier, the Shih Tzu, and the Lhasa Apso.

THE LHASA APSO IN AMERICA

This rare and unusual breed was introduced into the United States by Mr. and Mrs. C. Suydam Cutting. Mr. Cutting, a naturalist and friend of Theodore Roosevelt and his brother Kermit, was a member of the Roosevelt expedition to Chinese Turkistan in 1925, the prime objective being to collect specimens of animal life for U.S. museums. In 1928 Cutting accompanied the two Roosevelts to Chinese Tibet and participated in the hunt for the giant panda. Perhaps this brief peek into the backdoor of this mysterious and fascinating land prompted Cutting's later trips back into Tibet, and stimulated his interest sufficiently so that he persisted in trying to obtain permission to visit the city of Lhasa.

Tibet is one of the most inaccessible countries in the world, both by geography and by the insulated nature of this unique, non-Western culture. Therefore, an aura of mystery and powerful fascination exists about the country.

After the 1930 visit, Cutting began corresponding with His Holiness The 13th Dalai Lama of Tibet. Apparently this correspondence was very successful. Cutting was able to perform several official favors for the country of Tibet, and in the spring of 1931 he sent the Dalai Lama a pair of Dalmatians and a pair of German Shepherds. It is reported that Cutting was the only man with which the Dalai Lama kept up regular communications.

In Cutting's book *The Fire Ox and Other Years*, he writes the following: "In sending me a pair of Apsos (special breed of Tibetan dogs), the Dalai Lama wrote, 'I am sending you two dogs by way of Kalimpong. Please take good care of them when you receive them.' Dated 7th of the first Tibetan Month of the Water Bird Year."

This would have been sometime in the spring of 1933, since the Tibetan New Year varies, as does the Christians' Easter, but the first month begins sometime in March or April. And so, the first pair of *Bark, Sentinel Lion Dogs* reached the United States.

It is interesting to note that in February of the same year an article appeared in the *American Kennel Gazette* titled "Four Breeds of Dogs in Far Off Tibet," by

the shoulder as 11 inches, weight 20 pounds. She also indicates the dogs of 1933 varied greatly in size and came in colors of black, grizzle, smoke or sandy, but the most frequently seen was a mixture of these colors with white.

This delightful little Apso, owned by Miss M. Wild, is a direct descendant of dogs which had been presented to Chinese Emperors and noblemen by the Grand Dalai Lama.

Margaret Hayes. Apparently Mrs. Hayes lived for some years on the borders of Tibet and was very interested in Tibetan dogs. She calls one Tibetan breed the Tibetan Spaniel, which she classifies as a toy breed. Next in size, Mrs. Hayes indicates a breed called "Lhasa Terriers." She then goes on to say this dog is badly misnamed, being neither toy nor terrier. She speaks of a standard which was drawn up in 1901 which gives the height at

The next breed which Mrs. Hayes mentions is the "Apso," which she says is scarcer than the Lhasa Terrier, but is really the same breed, and owing to the scarceness of these beautifully honey-colored dogs, they had been given a name all to themselves. She describes the Apso as having a distinct mane of long hair around the neck, which gives it a lion-like appearance. And further goes on to say that the Tibetans call them "golden lion dog," and that their pet names in their Tibetan homes are often "singhi" (lion) or "singtukk" (lion cub).

Mrs. Hayes's next breed is what she calls the "Tibetan Terrier,"

same Baileys who were so prominent in popularizing Tibetan dogs in England.

Finally, in 1937, the Fire Ox Year, Mr. and Mrs. Cutting set out on their third and final trip to

For many years various types of dogs claiming to be Apsos were exhibited in English shows, but it was not until 1933 that the first genuine specimens made their appearance at the Ladies' Kennel Association Championship Show at Olympia. Here are two little dogs which made their debut on that occasion.

and she then goes on to describe the Tibetan Mastiff, a large guard dog, and the Corpse dogs, which are wild.

Before a third trip to Tibet could be organized, in 1936, Cutting and his wife received an invitation from the Lieutenant-Colonel F.M. Bailey, British Minister to Nepal, and Mrs. Bailey to visit and witness the 25th Jubilee of the King's Accession in Nepal. These, of course, were the

Tibet. They took the same route into Lhasa from India that Mr. Cutting had taken before. On the way to Lhasa near Lake Kala among a group of nomads Cutting tells us his wife saw the following, "In the throng my wife picked out a very good black-and-white Apso dog."

In Gyantse, the Cuttings were guests at the British fort. In the quarters of Rai Shahib Wangdi, Tibetan assistant to the British trade agent, they saw "three jet-black Apso dogs."

It was summer when the Cuttings reached Tibet, and the Regent was in residency at the summer palace, Norbu Linga. They met the Regent then and had tea with him and this is Cutting's description of their parting, "At parting, the ruler told my wife he would send her a pair of Apso dogs which greatly delighted her. I had received five of these dogs from the late Dalai Lama and started to breed them successfully in New Jersey. They are pure Tibetan breed, usually golden, blue-grey or black; to describe them I can only say that if a Pekingese were mated with a Yorkshire Terrier, the offspring would look like a first cousin of the Apso. The name, by the way, was registered outside of Tibet by Lieutenant-Colonel and Mrs. Bailey who introduced them to England."

The Cuttings stayed three weeks in Lhasa during which time they were entertained royally by the high government officials and the nobility. As they were leaving, Cutting noted that "the Regent kept his promise, and on the last day we received two golden Apsos, the dogs so much admired by the Tibetans." This pair, a male and female, rode out of Tibet with Mrs. Cutting and created quite a sensation along the route. A quantity of milk was presented to the travelers by the natives for the Apso dogs.

According to Cutting "the dogs rode well, especially Tsing Tu, the female, who bounced miraculously on my wife's saddle, mile after mile. A mile-and-a-half from every stop they would race ahead, chasing marmots."

A pair of Lhasa Apsos were sent to Mr. and Mrs. Cutting in 1950, by His Holiness The 14th Dalai Lama of Tibet. This was the last pair to be received before the Communist invasion.

In its native land of Tibet, the Lhasa Apso is known as *Apso Seng Kye* or "Bark, Sentinel Lion Dog."

YOUR LHASA APSO PUPPY

SELECTION

When you do pick out a Lhasa Apso puppy as a pet, don't be hasty; the longer you study puppies, the better you will understand them. Make it your transcendent concern to select only one that radiates good health and spirit and is lively on his feet, whose eyes are bright, whose coat shines, and who comes forward eagerly to make and to cultivate your acquaintance. Don't fall for any shy little darling that wants to retreat to his bed or his box, or plays coy behind other puppies or people, or hides his head under your arm or jacket appealing to your protective instinct. *Pick the Lhasa Apso puppy who forthrightly picks you! The feeling of attraction should be mutual!*

Owners should select for healthy-looking, outgoing Lhasa pups that are neither frail nor oversized. At eight weeks of age, Lhasa pups should weigh about 3$^1/_2$ pounds.

DOCUMENTS

Now, a little paper work is in order. When you purchase a purebred Lhasa Apso puppy, you should receive a transfer of ownership, registration material, and other "papers" (a list of the immunization shots, if any, the puppy may have been given; a note on whether or not the puppy has been wormed; a diet and feeding schedule to which the puppy is accustomed) and you are welcomed as a fellow owner to a long, pleasant association with a most lovable pet, and more (news)paper work.

GENERAL PREPARATION

You have chosen to own a particular Lhasa Apso puppy. You have chosen it very carefully over all other breeds and all other puppies. So before you ever get that Lhasa Apso puppy home,

Lhasa Apso puppies are cute and irresistible. Choosing just one is a difficult thing to do!

you will have prepared for its arrival by reading everything you can get your hands on having to do with the management of Lhasa Apsos and puppies. True, you will run into many conflicting opinions, but at least you will not be starting "blind." Read, study, digest. Talk over your plans with your veterinarian, other "Lhasa Apso people," and the seller of your Lhasa Apso puppy.

When you get your Lhasa Apso puppy, you will find that your reading and study are far from finished. You've just scratched the surface in your plan to provide the greatest possible comfort and health for your Lhasa Apso; and, by the same token, you do want to assure yourself of the greatest possible enjoyment of this wonderful creature. You must be ready for this puppy mentally as well as in the physical requirements.

TRANSPORTATION

If you take the puppy home by car, protect him from drafts, particularly in cold weather. Wrapped in a towel and carried in the arms or lap of a passenger,

When you transport your puppy home, protect him from drafts by wrapping him in warm blankets or towels.

the Lhasa Apso puppy will usually make the trip without mishap. If the pup starts to drool and to squirm, stop the car for a few minutes. Have newspapers handy in case of car-sickness. A covered carton lined with newspapers provides protection for puppy and car, if you are driving alone. Avoid excitement and unnecessary handling of the puppy on arrival. A Lhasa Apso puppy is a very small "package" to be making a complete change of surroundings and company, and he needs frequent rest and refreshment to renew his vitality.

THE FIRST DAY AND NIGHT

When your Lhasa Apso puppy arrives in your home, put him down on the floor and don't pick him up again, except when it is absolutely necessary. He is a dog, a real dog, and must not be lugged around like a rag doll. Handle him as little as possible, and permit no one to pick him up and baby him. To repeat, *put your Lhasa Apso puppy on the floor or the ground and let him stay there except when it may be necessary to do otherwise.*

Quite possibly your Lhasa Apso puppy will be afraid for a while in his new surroundings, without his mother and littermates. Comfort him and reassure him, but don't console him. Don't give him the "oh-you-poor-itsy-bitsy-puppy" treatment. Be calm, friendly, and reassuring. Encourage him to walk around and sniff over his new

Christmas puppy, when there is more excitement than usual and more chance for a puppy to swallow something upsetting. It is a better plan to welcome the puppy several days before or after the holiday week. Like a baby, your Lhasa Apso puppy needs

In a single litter you will find that some puppies are more active and curious than others. If possible, take time to observe the entire litter to choose the puppy with the personality that best suits your lifestyle.

home. If it's dark, put on the lights. Let him roam for a few minutes while you and everyone else concerned sit quietly or go about your routine business. Let the puppy come back to you.

Playmates may cause an immediate problem if the new Lhasa Apso puppy is to be greeted by children or other pets. If not, you can skip this subject. The natural affinity between puppies and children calls for some supervision until a live-and-let-live relationship is established. This applies particularly to a

much rest and should not be over-handled. Once a child realizes that a puppy has "feelings" similar to his own, and can readily be hurt or injured, the opportunities for play and responsibilities provide exercise and training for both.

For his first night with you, he should be put where he is to sleep every night—say in the kitchen, since its floor can usually be easily cleaned. Let him explore the kitchen to his heart's content; close doors to confine him there. Prepare his food and feed him lightly the first night. Give him a pan with some water in it—not a lot, since most puppies will try to drink the whole pan dry. Give him an old coat or shirt to lie on. Since a coat or shirt will be strong in human scent, he will pick it out to lie on, thus furthering his feeling of security in the room where he has just been fed.

HOUSEBREAKING HELPS

Now, sooner or later—mostly sooner—your new Lhasa Apso puppy is going to "puddle" on the floor. First take a newspaper and lay it on the puddle until the

During the initial stages of housebreaking, water should only be offered to the pup at certain times.

Many breeders use newspaper as the lining for their litter's crate. If this is the case with your new Lhasa, it will make paper training easier because the pup will already be familiar with eliminating on newspaper.

urine is soaked up onto the paper. *Save this paper.* Now take a cloth with soap and water, wipe up the floor and dry it well. Then take the wet paper and place it on a fairly large square of newspapers in a convenient corner. When cleaning up, always keep a piece of wet paper on top of the others. Every time he wants to "squat," he will seek out this spot and use the papers. (This routine is rarely necessary for more than three days.) Now leave your Lhasa Apso puppy for the night. Quite probably he will cry and howl a bit; some are more stubborn than others on this matter. But let him stay alone for the night. This may seem harsh treatment, but it is the best procedure in the long run. Just let him cry; he will weary of it sooner or later.

FEEDING

Now let's talk about feeding your Lhasa Apso, a subject so simple that it's amazing there is so much nonsense and misunderstanding about it. Is it expensive to feed a Lhasa Apso? No, it is not! You can feed your Lhasa Apso economically and keep him in perfect shape the "picky" eaters) they will eat almost anything that they become accustomed to. Many dogs flatly refuse to eat nice, fresh beef. They pick around it and eat everything else. But meat—bah! Why? They aren't accustomed to it! They'd eat rabbit fast enough, but they

It is best to feed your new Lhasa puppy the same food he was eating before you brought him home. Any change in food should be made gradually.

year round, or you can feed him expensively. He'll thrive either way, and let's see why this is true.

First of all, remember a Lhasa Apso is a dog. Dogs do not have a high degree of selectivity in their food, and unless you spoil them with great variety (and possibly turn them into poor, refuse beef because they aren't used to it.

VARIETY NOT NECESSARY

A good general rule of thumb is forget all human preferences and don't give a thought to variety. Choose the right diet for your Lhasa Apso and feed it to him day after day, year after year,

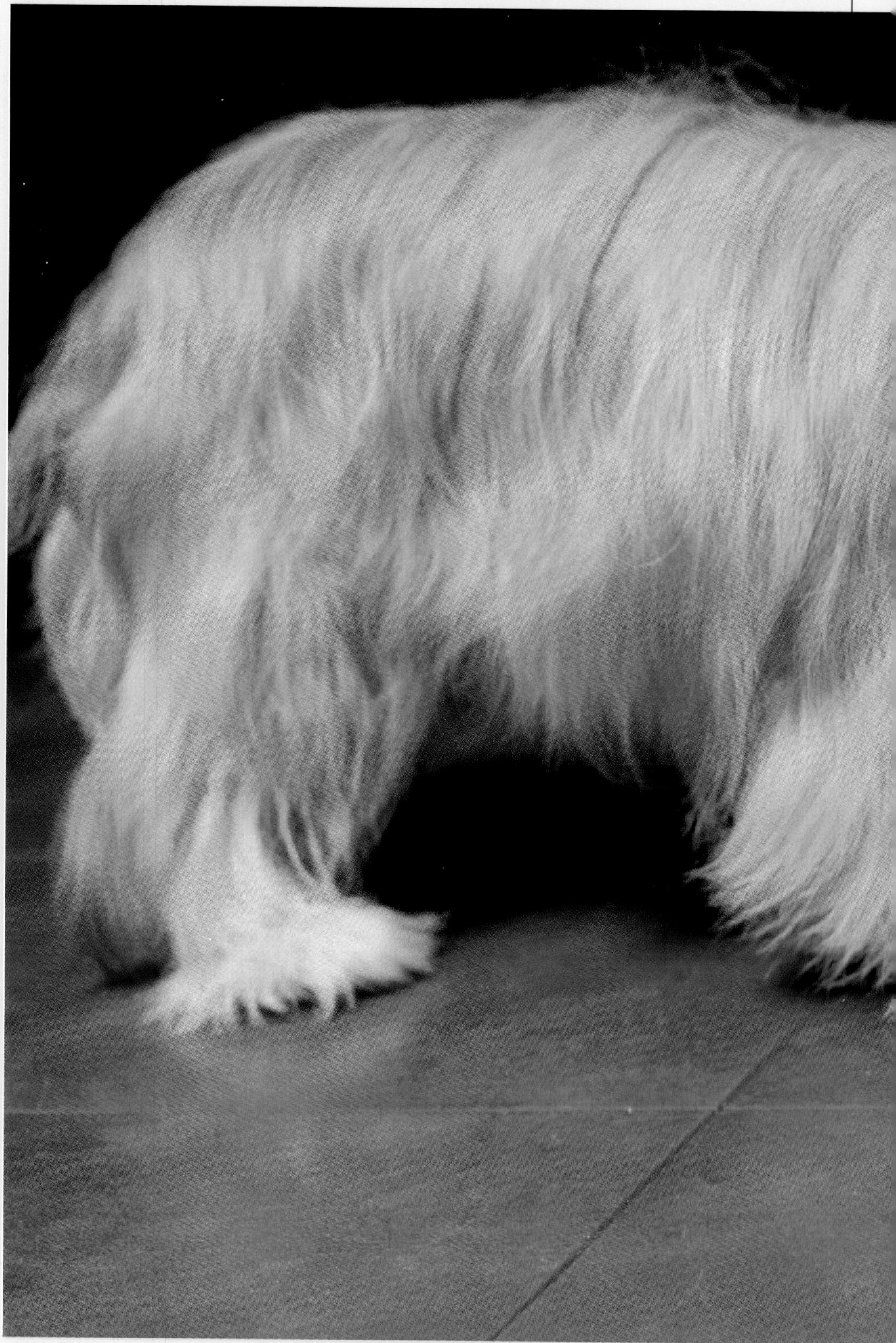

Some owners like to tie up their Lhasas' facial hair to keep it from falling into their food dishes while they are eating. This Lhasa, however, won't let a little hair get in the way of his dinner!

winter and summer. But what is the right diet?

Hundreds of thousands of dollars have been spent in canine nutrition research. The results are pretty conclusive, so you needn't go into a lot of experimenting with trials of this and that every other week. Research has proven just what your dog needs to eat and to keep healthy.

DOG FOOD

There are almost as many right diets as there are dog experts, but the basic diet most often recommended is one that consists of a dry food, either meal or kibble form. There are several of excellent quality, manufactured by reliable

For no-mess feeding, a feeding tray is very practical. Feeding trays are available in different styles and colors at your local pet shop. Photo courtesy of Penn Plax.

companies, research tested, and nationally advertised. They are inexpensive, highly satisfactory, and easily available in stores everywhere in containers of five to 50 pounds. Larger amounts cost less per pound, usually.

If you have a choice of brands, it is usually safer to choose the better known one; but even so, carefully read the analysis on the package. Do not choose any food in which the protein level is less than 25 percent, and be sure that

this protein comes from both animal and vegetable sources. The good dog foods have meat meal, fish meal, liver, and such, plus protein from alfalfa and soy beans, as well as some dried-milk product. Note the vitamin content carefully. See that they are all there in good proportions; and be especially certain that the food contains properly high levels of vitamins A and D, two of the most perishable and important ones. Note the B-complex level, but don't worry about carbohydrate and mineral levels. These substances are plentiful and cheap and not likely to be lacking in a good brand.

The advice given for how to choose a dry food also applies to moist or canned types of dog foods, if you decide to feed one of these.

Having chosen a really good food, feed it to your Lhasa Apso as the manufacturer directs. And once you've started, stick to it. Never change if you can possibly help it. A switch from one meal or kibble-type food can usually be made without too much upset; however, a change will almost invariably give you (and your Lhasa Apso) some trouble.

WHEN SUPPLEMENTS ARE NEEDED

Now what about supplements of various kinds, mineral and vitamin, or the various oils? They are all okay to add to your Lhasa Apso's food. However, if you are feeding your Lhasa Apso a correct diet, and this is easy to do, no supplements are necessary unless your Lhasa Apso has been improperly fed, has been sick, or is having puppies. Vitamins and minerals are naturally present in all the foods; and to ensure against any loss through processing, they are added in concentrated form to the dog food you use. Except on the advice of your veterinarian, added amounts of vitamins can prove harmful to your Lhasa Apso! The same risk goes with minerals.

FEEDING SCHEDULE

When and how much food to give your Lhasa Apso? As to when (except in the instance of puppies), suit yourself. You may feed two meals per day or the same amount in one single feeding, either morning or night. As to how to prepare the food and how much to give, it is generally best to follow the directions on the food package. Your own Lhasa Apso may want a little more or a little less.

Fresh, cool water should always be available to your Lhasa Apso. This is important to good health throughout his lifetime.

Your Lhasa Apso will come to love his Nylabones® so much that he will do anything for one.

ALL LHASA APSOS NEED TO CHEW

Puppies and young Lhasa Apsos need something with resistance to chew on while their teeth and jaws are developing—for cutting the puppy teeth, to induce growth of the permanent teeth under the puppy teeth, to assist in getting rid of the puppy teeth at the proper time, to help the permanent teeth through the gums, to ensure normal jaw development, and to settle the permanent teeth solidly in the jaws.

The adult Lhasa Apso's desire to chew stems from the instinct for tooth cleaning, gum massage, and jaw exercise—plus the need for an outlet for periodic doggie tensions.

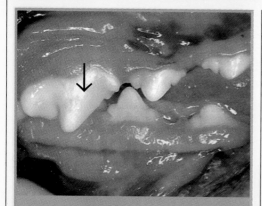

A scientific study, shows a dog's tooth (arrow) while being maintained by Gumabone® chewing.

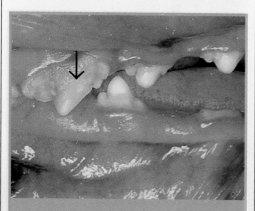

The Gumabone® was taken away and in 30 days the tooth (arrow) was almost completely covered with plaque and tartar.

This is why dogs, especially puppies and young dogs, will often destroy property worth hundreds of dollars when their chewing instinct is not diverted from their owner's possessions. And this is why you should provide your Lhasa Apso with something to chew—something that has the necessary functional qualities, is desirable from the Lhasa Apso's viewpoint, and is safe for him.

It is very important that your Lhasa Apso not be permitted to chew on anything he can break or on any indigestible thing from which he can bite sizable chunks. Sharp pieces, such as from a bone which can be broken by a dog, may pierce the intestinal wall and kill. Indigestible things that can be bitten off in chunks, such as from shoes or rubber or plastic toys, may cause an intestinal stoppage (if not regurgitated) and bring painful death, unless surgery is promptly performed.

Strong natural bones, such as 4- to 8-inch lengths of round shin bone from mature beef—either the kind you can get from a butcher or one of the variety available commercially in pet stores—may serve your Lhasa Apso's teething needs if his mouth is large enough to handle them effectively. You may be tempted to give your Lhasa Apso puppy a smaller bone and he may not be able to break it when you do, but puppies grow

Pet shops sell real bones that have been colored, cooked, dyed or served natural. These are less safe than nylon bones.

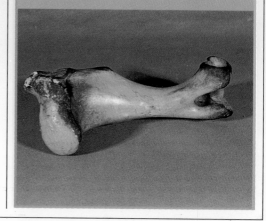

rapidly and the power of their jaws constantly increases until maturity. This means that a growing Lhasa Apso may break one of the smaller bones at any time, swallow the pieces, and die painfully before you realize what is wrong.

All hard natural bones are very abrasive. If your Lhasa Apso is an avid chewer, natural bones may wear away his teeth prematurely; hence, they then should be taken away from your dog when the teething purposes have been served. The badly worn, and usually painful, teeth of many mature dogs can be traced to excessive chewing on natural bones.

Contrary to popular belief, knuckle bones that can be chewed up and swallowed by your Lhasa Apso provide little, if any,

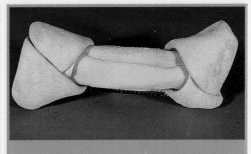

Rawhide is probably the best-selling dog chew. It can be dangerous and cause a dog to choke on it, as it swells when wet.

usable calcium or other nutrient. They do, however, disturb the digestion of most dogs and cause them to vomit the nourishing food they need.

Dried rawhide products of various types, shapes, sizes, and prices are available on the market and have become quite popular. However, they don't serve the

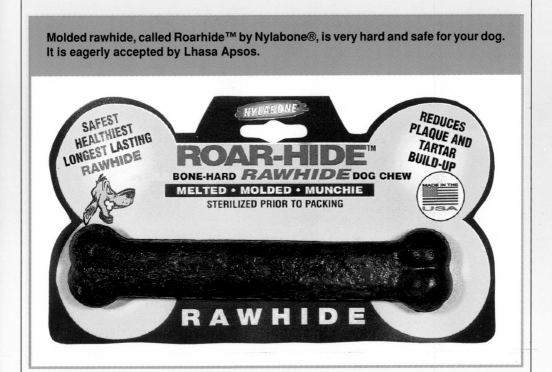

Molded rawhide, called Roarhide™ by Nylabone®, is very hard and safe for your dog. It is eagerly accepted by Lhasa Apsos.

A Gumabone® after chewing. The knobs develop elastic frays that act as a toothbrush.

A new product, molded rawhide, is very safe. During the process, the rawhide is melted and then injection molded into the familiar dog shape. It is very hard and is eagerly accepted by Lhasa Apsos. The melting process also sterilizes the rawhide. Don't confuse this with pressed rawhide, which is nothing more than small strips of rawhide squeezed together.

The nylon bones, especially those with natural meat and bone fractions added, are probably the most complete, safe, and economical answer to the chewing need. Dogs cannot break them or bite off sizable chunks; hence, they are completely safe—

The Nylafloss® tug-toy is actually a dental floss. You grab one end and let your Lhasa Apso pull at the other as it slowly slips through his teeth since nylon is self-lubricating.

primary chewing functions very well; they are a bit messy when wet from mouthing, and most Lhasa Apsos chew them up rather rapidly—but they have been considered safe for dogs until recently. Now, more and more incidents of death, and near death, by strangulation have been reported to be the results of partially swallowed chunks of rawhide swelling in the throat. More recently, some veterinarians have been attributing cases of acute constipation to large pieces of incompletely digested rawhide in the intestine.

and being longer lasting than other things offered for the purpose, they are economical.

Hard chewing raises little bristle-like projections on the surface of the nylon bones—to provide effective interim tooth cleaning and vigorous gum massage, much in the same way your toothbrush does it for you. The little projections are raked off and swallowed in the form of thin shavings, but the chemistry of the nylon is such that they break down in the stomach fluids and pass through without effect.

The toughness of the nylon provides the strong chewing resistance needed for important jaw exercise and effectively aids teething functions, but there is no tooth wear because nylon is non-abrasive. Being inert, nylon does not support the growth of microorganisms; and it can be washed in soap and water or it can be sterilized by boiling or in an autoclave.

Nylabone® is highly recommended by veterinarians as a safe, healthy nylon bone that can't splinter or chip. Nylabone® is frizzled by the dog's chewing action, creating a toothbrush-like surface that cleanses the teeth and massages the gums. Nylabone®, the only chew products made of flavor-impregnated solid nylon, are available in your local pet shop. Nylabone® is superior to the cheaper bones because it is made of virgin nylon, which is the strongest and longest-lasting type of nylon available. The cheaper bones are made from recycled or re-ground nylon scraps, and have a tendency to break apart and split easily.

Nothing, however, substitutes for periodic professional attention for your Lhasa Apso's teeth and gums, not any more than your toothbrush can do that for you. Have your Lhasa Apso's teeth cleaned at least once a year by your veterinarian (twice a year is better) and he will be happier, healthier, and far more pleasant to live with.

There are special bones made just for puppies. They usually are filled with calcium supplements and are very hard. The most popular of the puppy bones is the one made by Nylabone®.

TRAINING

You owe proper training to your Lhasa Apso. The right and privilege of being trained is his birthright; and whether your Lhasa Apso is going to be a quietly at "Heel," whether on or off lead. He must be mannerly and polite wherever he goes; he must be polite to strangers on the street and in stores. He

The key to training is consistency. Don't let your puppy do things that he will not be allowed to do as an adult, such as sitting on the furniture.

handsome, well-mannered housedog and companion, a show dog, or whatever possible use he may be put to, the basic training is always the same—all must start with basic obedience, or what might be called "manner training."

Your Lhasa Apso must come instantly when called and obey the "Sit" or "Down" command just as fast; he must walk must be mannerly in the presence of other dogs. He must not bark at children on roller skates, motorcycles, or other domestic animals. And he must be restrained from chasing cats. It is not a dog's inalienable right to chase cats, and he must be reprimanded for it.

PROFESSIONAL TRAINING

How do you go about this

training? Well, it's a very simple procedure, pretty well standardized by now. First, if you can afford the extra expense, you may send your Lhasa Apso to a professional trainer, where in 30 to 60 days he will learn how to be a "good dog." If you enlist the services of a good professional trainer, follow his advice of when to come to see the dog. No, he won't forget you, but too-frequent visits at the wrong time may slow down his training progress. And using a "pro" trainer means that you will have to go for some training, too, after the trainer feels your Lhasa Apso is ready to go home. You will have to learn how your Lhasa Apso works, just what to expect of him and how to use what the dog has learned after he is home.

OBEDIENCE TRAINING CLASS

Another way to train your Lhasa Apso (many experienced Lhasa Apso people think this is the best) is to join an obedience training class right in your own community. There is such a group in nearly every community nowadays. Here you will be working with a group of people who are also just starting out. You will actually be training your own dog, since all work is done under the direction of a head trainer who will make suggestions to you and also tell you when and how to correct your Lhasa Apso's errors. Then, too, working with such a group, your Lhasa Apso will learn to get along with other dogs. And, what is more important, he will learn to do exactly what he is told to do, no matter how much confusion there is around him or how great the temptation is to go his own way.

Write to your national kennel club for the location of a training club or class in your locality. Sign up. Go to it regularly— every session! Go early and leave late! Both you and your Lhasa Apso will benefit tremendously.

Basic obedience training should begin when your Lhasa Apso is still a young puppy. If you make the training sessions short and enjoyable, the puppy will look forward to them.

TRAIN HIM BY THE BOOK

The third way of training your Lhasa Apso is by the book. Yes, you can do it this way and do a good job of it too. But in using the book method, select a book, buy it, study it carefully; then study it some more, until the procedures are almost second nature to you. Then start your training. But stay with the book and its advice and exercises. Don't start in and then make up a few rules of your own. If you don't follow the book, you'll get into jams you can't get out of by yourself. If after a few hours of short training sessions your Lhasa Apso is still not working as he should, get back to the book

Successful Dog Training is one of the better books by which you can train your Lhasa Apso. The author, Michael Kamer, trains dogs for Hollywood stars and movies.

Some owners who have fenced yards can train their Lhasas to use a pet-door to go in and out of the house whenever they please. Young puppies can be trained to use this device but should still be supervised when they are outside.

for a study session, because it's your fault, not the dog's! The procedures of dog training have been so well systemized that it must be your fault, since literally thousands of fine Lhasa Apsos have been trained by the book.

After your Lhasa Apso is "letter perfect" under all conditions, then, if you wish, go on to advanced training and trick work.

Your Lhasa Apso will love his obedience training, and you'll burst with pride at the finished product! Your Lhasa Apso will enjoy life even more, and you'll enjoy your Lhasa Apso more. And remember—you *owe good training to your Lhasa Apso.*

SHOWING YOUR LHASA APSO

A show Lhasa Apso is a comparatively rare thing. He is one out of several litters of puppies. He happens to be born with a degree of physical perfection that closely approximates the standard by which the breed is judged in the show ring. Such a dog should, on maturity, be able to win or approach his championship in good, fast company at the larger shows. Upon finishing his championship, he is apt to be as highly desirable as a breeding animal. As a proven stud, he will automatically command a high price for service.

Showing Lhasa Apsos is a lot of fun—yes, but it is a highly competitive sport. While all the experts were once beginners, the odds are against a novice. You will be showing against experienced handlers, often people who have devoted a lifetime to breeding, picking the right ones, and then showing those dogs through to their championships.

1995 Westminster Best of Breed Winner Ch. Hoshira Hylan Shotru Brie owned by Michael A. Santora and Alan J. Loso. Westminster is the most prestigious dog show in the United States.

Moreover, the most perfect Lhasa Apso ever born has faults, and in your hands the faults will be far more evident than with the experienced handler who knows how to minimize his Lhasa Apso's faults. These are but a few points on the sad side of the picture.

The experienced handler, as I say, was not born knowing the ropes. He learned— *and so can you!* You can if you will put in the same time, study and keen observation that he did. But it will take time!

KEY TO SUCCESS

First, search for a truly fine show prospect. Take the puppy home, raise him by the book, and as carefully as you know how, give him every chance to mature into the Lhasa Apso you hoped for. My advice is to keep your dog out of big shows, even Puppy Classes, until he is mature. Maturity in the male is roughly two years; with the female, 14 months or so. When your Lhasa Apso is approaching maturity, start out at match shows, and, with this experience for both of you, then go gunning for the big wins at the big shows.

Next step, read the standard by which the Lhasa Apso is judged. Study it until you know it by heart. Having done this, and while your puppy is at home (where he should be) growing into a normal, healthy Lhasa Apso, go to every dog show you can possibly reach. Sit at the ringside and watch Lhasa Apso judging. Keep your ears and eyes open. Do your own judging, holding each of those dogs against the standard, which you now know by heart.

In your evaluations, don't start looking for faults. Look for the virtues—the best qualities. How does a given Lhasa Apso shape up against the standard? Having looked for and noted the virtues, then note the faults and see what prevents a given Lhasa Apso from standing correctly or moving well. Weigh these faults against the virtues, since, ideally, every feature of the dog should

Although showing your Lhasa Apso is fun, it is a lot of work. You must learn how to show your dog to his best advantage.

The ideal Lhasa Apso show prospect conforms very closely to the standard. This Lhasa exhibits excellent conformation.

contribute to the harmonious whole dog.

"RINGSIDE JUDGING"

It's a good practice to make notes on each Lhasa Apso, always holding the dog against the standard. In "ringside judging," forget your personal preference for this or that feature. What does the standard say about it? Watch carefully as the judge places the dogs in a given class. It is difficult from the ringside always to see why number one was placed over the second dog. Try to follow the judge's reasoning. Later try to talk with the judge after he is finished. Ask him questions as to why he placed certain Lhasa Apsos and not others. Listen while the judge explains his placings, and, I'll say right here, any judge worthy of his license should be able to give reasons.

When you're not at the ringside, talk with the fanciers and breeders who have Lhasa Apsos. Don't be afraid to ask opinions or say that you don't know. You have a lot of listening to do, and it will help you a great deal and speed up your personal progress if you are a good listener.

THE NATIONAL CLUB

You will find it worthwhile to join the national Lhasa Apso club and to subscribe to its magazine. From the national club, you will learn the location of an approved regional club near you. Now, when your young Lhasa Apso is eight to ten months old, find out the dates of match shows in your section of the country. These differ from regular shows only in that no championship points are given. These shows are especially designed to launch young dogs (and new handlers) on a show career.

what he may want you to do next. Watch only the judge and your Lhasa Apso. Be quick and be alert; do exactly as the judge directs. Don't speak to him except to answer his questions. If he does something you don't like, don't say so. And don't irritate the judge (and everybody else) by constantly talking and fussing

This Lhasa was a winner at the 1990 World Dog Show. This show is held annually in a different city each year.

ENTER MATCH SHOWS

With the ring deportment you have watched at big shows firmly in mind and practice, enter your Lhasa Apso in as many match shows as you can. When in the ring, you have two jobs. One is to see to it that your Lhasa Apso is always being seen to its best advantage. The other job is to keep your eye on the judge to see

with your dog.

In moving about the ring, remember to keep clear of dogs beside you or in front of you. It is my advice to you *not* to show your Lhasa Apso in a regular point show until he is at least close to maturity and after both you and your dog have had time to perfect ring manners and poise in the match shows.

YOUR LHASA APSO'S HEALTH

We know our pets, their moods and habits, and therefore we can recognize when our Lhasa Apso is experiencing an off-day. Signs of sickness can be very obvious or very subtle. As any mother can next to you. It will pay to be choosy about your veterinarian. Talk to dog-owning friends whom you respect. Visit more than one vet before you make a lifelong choice. Trust your instincts. Find

Grooming for good health makes good sense. The Apso's outer coat benefits from regular brushing to keep looking glossy and clean.

attest, diagnosing and treating an ailment require common sense, knowing when to seek home remedies and when to visit your doctor...or veterinarian, as the case may be.

Your veterinarian, we know, is your Lhasa Apso's best friend, a knowledgeable, compassionate vet who knows Lhasa Apsos and likes them.

Grooming for good health makes good sense. The Apso's outer coat is heavy and straight and benefits from regular brushing to keep looking glossy and clean. Brushing stimulates the natural oils in the coat and also removes dead haircoat. The Apso's coat is more like human hair than like dog fur: it is a single coat which means it does not shed like most other dogs. Puppies require additional grooming to usher in the impressive and heavy adult coat. Apso's may be prone to skin irritations too, so grooming

accumulates so you can readily feel these structures from the outside. If your Lhasa Apso is scooting across the floor dragging his rear quarters, or licking his rear, his anal sacs may need to be expressed. Placing pressure in and up towards the anus, while holding the tail, is the general routine.

Anal sac secretions are

It is important to maintain your Lhasa Apso's health from puppyhood through adulthood.

can help minimize any potential skin maladies.

ANAL SACS

Anal sacs, sometimes called anal glands, are located in the musculature of the anal ring, one on either side. Each empties into the rectum via a small duct. Occasionally their secretion becomes thickened and

characteristically foul-smelling, and you could get squirted if not careful. Veterinarians can take care of this during regular visits and demonstrate the cleanest method.

MAJOR HEALTH ISSUES

Many Lhasa Apsos are predisposed to certain congenital and inherited abnormalities, such as hip dysplasia, which has become more common in Apsos in recent years. Fortunately it doesn't plague the Apso as it does most large breeds of dog. New owners should insist on screening certificates from such hip registries as OFA or PennHIP. Since HD is hereditary, it's necessary to know that the parents and grandparents of your puppy had hips rated good or better. Dysplastic dogs suffer from badly constructed hip joints which become arthritic and very painful, thereby hindering the dog's ability to be a working dog, a good-moving show dog, or even a happy, active pet.

Eye conditions such as distichiasis and progressive retinal atrophy (PRA) have become concerns for Apso breeders. Screening for eye problems has therefore been prioritized. PRA is an inherited defect that can severely reduce a dog's vision. Distichiasis (extra eyelashes) can be corrected through surgery though eliminate the dog from competing in dog shows. Eye ulcers and kerato conjunctivitis sicca (commonly called "dry eye") appear in many short-faced dogs. Dry eye results from the lachrymal glands producing less and less tears. It is not clear whether this condition results hereditarily in every case or from environmental or physical conditions (thyroid, immune system, etc.).

Some Apsos are prone to kidney disease in its most common form, chronic renal failure, which occurs over a period of time. Older dogs of all breeds experience less-efficient kidney function which is not the same. Acute kidney failure requires immediate veterinary diagnosis and treatment.

Keep your puppy close to home until he's had all of his inoculations. As soon as this little pup is fully vaccinated he will be able to see what is on the other side of that fence.

VACCINATIONS

For the continued health of your dog, owners must attend to vaccinations regularly. Your veterinarian can recommend a vaccination schedule appropriate for your dog, taking into consideration the factors of climate and geography. The basic vaccinations to protect your dog

Although the long coat of the Lhasa Apso is luxurious, it is a lot of work. Mats and tangles in the coat can be very problematic: if you cannot commit to brushing your dog daily, you may want to consider clipping the coat shorter.

are: parvovirus, distemper, hepatitis, leptospirosis, adenovirus, parainfluenza, coronavirus, bordetella, tracheobronchitis (kennel cough), Lyme disease and rabies.

Parvovirus is a highly contagious, dog-specific disease, first recognized in 1978. Targeting the small intestine, parvo affects the stomach, and diarrhea and vomiting (with blood) are clinical signs. Although the dog can pass the infection to other dogs within three days of infection, the initial signs, which include lethargy and depression, don't display themselves until four to seven days. When affecting puppies under four weeks of age, the heart muscle is frequently attacked. When the heart is affected, the puppies exhibit difficulty in breathing and experience crying and foaming at the nose and mouth.

Distemper, related to human measles, is an airborne virus that spreads in the blood and ultimately in the nervous system and epithelial tissues. Young dogs or dogs with weak immune systems can develop encephalomyelitis (brain disease) from the distemper infection. Such dogs experience seizures, general weakness and rigidity, as well as "hardpad." Since distemper is largely incurable, prevention through vaccination is vitally important. Puppies should be vaccinated at six to eight weeks of age, with boosters at ten to 12 weeks. Older puppies (16 weeks and older) who are unvaccinated should receive no fewer than two vaccinations at three- to four-week intervals.

Hepatitis mainly affects the liver and is caused by canine adenovirus type I. Highly infectious, hepatitis often affects dogs nine to 12 months of age. Initially the virus localizes in the dog's tonsils and then disperses to the liver, kidneys and eyes. Generally speaking the dog's immune system is capable of combating this virus. Canine infectious hepatitis affects dogs whose systems cannot fight off the adenovirus. Affected dogs have fever, abdominal pains, bruising on mucous membranes and gums, and experience coma and convulsions. Prevention of hepatitis exists only through vaccination at eight to ten weeks of age and then boosters three or four weeks later, then annually.

Leptospirosis is a bacterium-related disease, often spread by rodents. The organisms that spread leptospirosis enter through the mucous membranes and spread to the internal organs via the bloodstream. It can be passed through the dog's urine. Leptospirosis does not affect young dogs as consistently as the other viruses; it is reportedly regional in distribution and somewhat dependent on the immunostatus of the dog. Fever, inappetence, vomiting, dehydration, hemorrhage, kidney and eye disease can result in moderate cases.

Bordetella, called canine cough, causes a persistent hacking cough in dogs and is very contagious. Bordetella involves a

The Lhasa Apso's eyefall protects his eyes against the glare of the sun and dust.

virus and a bacteria: parainfluenza is the most common virus implicated; *Bordetella bronchiseptica*, the bacterium. Bronchitis and pneumonia result in less than 20 percent of the cases, and most dogs recover from the condition within a week to four weeks. Non-prescription medicines can help relieve the hacking cough, though nothing can cure the condition before it's run its course. Vaccination cannot guarantee protection from canine cough, but it does ward off the most common virus responsible for the condition.

Lyme disease (also called borreliosis), although known for decades, was only first diagnosed in dogs in 1984. Lyme disease can affect cats, cattle, and horses, but especially people. In the U.S., the disease is transmitted by two ticks carrying the *Borrelia burgdorferi* organism: the deer tick (*Ixodes*

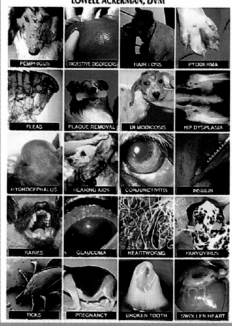

The undisputed champion of dog health books is Dr. Lowell Ackerman's encyclopedic work *Owner's Guide to DOG HEALTH*. It covers every subject that any dog owner might need. It actually is a complete veterinarian's handbook in simple, easy-to-understand language.

Plenty of fresh air and exercise will keep your Lhasa healthy and happy.

scapularis) and the western black-legged tick (*Ixodes pacificus*), the latter primarily affects reptiles. In Europe, *Ixodes ricinus* is responsible for spreading Lyme. The disease causes lameness, fever, joint swelling, inappetence, and lethargy. Removal of ticks from the dog's coat can help reduce the chances of Lyme, though not as much as avoiding heavily wooded areas where the dog is most likely to contract ticks.

A vaccination is available, though it has not been proven to protect dogs from all strains of the organism that cause the disease.

Rabies is passed to dogs and people through wildlife: in North America, principally through the skunk, fox and raccoon; the bat is not the culprit it was once thought to be. Likewise, the common image of the rabid dog foaming at the mouth with every hair on end is unlikely the truest commonly euthanized. Puppies are generally vaccinated at 12 weeks of age, and then annually. Although rabies is on the decline in the world community, tens of thousands of humans die each year from rabies-related incidents.

COPING WITH PARASITES

Parasites have clung to our pets for centuries. Despite our modern efforts, fleas still pester our pet's existence, and our own. All dogs

Well-bred Lhasa Apsos are healthy, long-lived companion animals.

scenario. A rabid dog exhibits difficulty eating, salivates much and has spells of paralysis and awkwardness. Before a dog reaches this final state, it may experience anxiety, personality changes, irritability and more aggressiveness than is usual. Vaccinations are strongly recommended as rabid dogs are too dangerous to manage and are itch, and fleas can make even the happiest dog a miserable, scabby mess. The loss of hair and habitual biting and chewing at themselves rank among the annoyances; the nuisances include the passing of tapeworms and the whole family's itching through the summer months. A full range of flea-control and elimination products are available at pet shops, and your veterinarian surely has recommendations. Sprays, powders, collars and dips fight fleas from the outside; drops and pills fight the good fight from inside. Discuss the possibilities with your vet. Not all products can be used in conjunction with one another, and some dogs may be more sensitive to certain applications than others. The dog's living quarters must be debugged as well as the dog itself. Heavy infestation may require multiple treatments.

Always check your dog for ticks carefully. Although fleas can be acquired almost anywhere, ticks are more likely to be picked up in heavily treed areas, pastures or other outside grounds (such as dog shows or obedience or field trials). Athletic, active, and hunting dogs are the most likely subjects, though any passing dog can be the host. Remember Lyme disease is passed by tick infestation.

As for internal parasites, worms are potentially dangerous for dogs and people. Roundworms, hookworms, whipworms, tapeworms, and heartworms comprise the blightsome party of troublemakers. Deworming puppies begins at around two to three weeks and continues until three months of age. Proper hygienic care of the environment is also important to prevent contamination with roundworm and hookworm eggs. Heartworm preventatives are recommended by most veterinarians, although there are some drawbacks to the regular introduction of poisons into our

dogs' system. These daily or monthly preparations also help regulate most other worms as well. Discuss worming procedures with your veterinarian.

Roundworms pose a great threat to dogs and people. They are found in the intestines of dogs, and can be passed to people through ingestion of feces-contaminated dirt. Roundworm infection can be prevented by not walking dogs in heavy-traffic people areas, by burning feces, and by curbing dogs in a responsible manner. (Of course, in most areas of the country, curbing dogs is the law.) Roundworms are typically passed from the bitch to the litter, and the bitch should be treated along with the puppies, even if she tested negative prior to whelping. Generally puppies are treated every two weeks until two months of age.

Hookworms, like roundworms, are also a danger to dogs and people. The hookworm parasite (known as *Ancylostoma caninum*) causes cutaneous larva migrans in people. The eggs of hookworms are passed in feces and become infective in shady, sandy areas. The larvae penetrate the skin of the dog, and the dog subsequently becomes infected. When swallowed, these parasites affect the intestines, lungs, windpipe, and the whole digestive system. Infected dogs suffer from anemia and lose large amounts of blood in the places where the worms latch onto the dog's intestines, etc.

Although infrequently passed to humans, whipworms are cited as one of the most common parasites in America. These elongated

Proper care and education can only help owners promote the health and longevity of their Lhasa Apsos.

worms affect the intestines of the dog, where they latch on, and cause colic upset or diarrhea. Unless identified in stools passed, whipworms are difficult to diagnose. Adult worms can be eliminated more consistently than the larvae, since whipworms exhibit unusual life cycles. Proper hygienic care of outdoor grounds is critical to the avoidance of these harmful parasites.

Tapeworms are carried by fleas, and enter the dog when the dog swallows the flea. Humans can acquire tapeworms in the same way, though we are less likely to swallow fleas than dogs are. Recent studies have shown that certain rodents and wild animals

have been infected with tapeworms, and dogs can be affected by catching and/or eating these other animals. Of course, outdoor hunting dogs and terriers are more likely to be infected in this way than are your typical house dog or non-motivated hound. Treatment for tapeworm has proven very effective, and infected dogs do not show great discomfort or symptoms. When people are infected, however, the liver can be

seriously damaged. Proper cleanliness is the best bet against tapeworms.

Heartworm disease is transmitted by mosquitoes and badly affects the lungs, heart and blood vessels of dogs. The larvae of *Dirofilaria immitis* enters the dog's bloodstream when bitten by an infected mosquito. The larvae takes about six months to mature. Infected dogs suffer from weight loss, appetite loss, chronic coughing and general fatigue. Not all affected dogs show signs of illness right away, and carrier dogs may be affected for years before clinical signs appear. Treatment of heartworm disease has been effective

After your Lhasa has come in from outdoors, especially grassy or heavily treed areas, check his coat for fleas and ticks.

but can be dangerous also. Prevention as always is the desirable alternative. Ivermectin is the active ingredient in most heartworm preventatives and has proven to be successful. Check with your veterinarian for the preparation best for your dog. Dogs generally begin taking the preventatives at eight months of age and continue to do so throughout the non-winter months.

GROOMING THE LHASA APSO

BASIC RULES

The grooming of an Apso can be as easy or as hard as you make it. There are a few simple rules to follow that will take some of the headaches out of

the Lhasa should never be bathed unless he has been brushed thoroughly. If a Lhasa is bathed without brushing, he will come out of his bath with some very incorrigible mats.

A beautifully groomed Lhasa Apso is a sight to behold!

grooming. First, the dog should never be brushed dry. The coat should be sprayed with a coat dressing, or plain water from a spray-nozzled dispenser. The coat should be slightly dampened and then brushed with a bristle brush until dry. The dampening of the coat will help prevent it from breaking off. Also, and most important,

However, if mats should be encountered, rather than cutting them out, commercial coat oil made especially for pets, should be applied to the mat, allowed to soak in and then the mat will comb out easily.

GROOMING BEHAVIOR

When introducing a puppy to grooming, do so gently. Place

Many Lhasa Apso owners prefer to hold the eyefall up with elastic bands or barrettes, so they can see the lovely expression in the eyes of their pets.

starting, with whatever preparation you are using, and then brush gently, parting the hair and brushing it in layers from the skin to the tips of the coat. When you finish the stomach and chest, turn him on each side in turn so you can do the heavy coat along the sides of the hocks and the body. Still continue to part the hair and brush it in layers. Then allow him to lie right side up on the table, part his coat down the middle from the tip of his nose to the base of his tail, smooth down the longer outer coat, brush the tail, and very carefully with a fine-toothed comb, smooth down his whiskers and

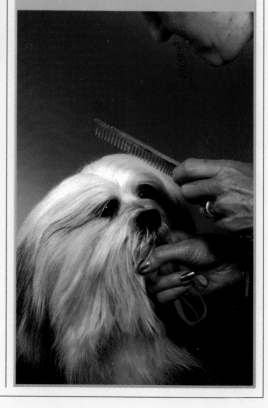

Use a steel-toothed comb around your Lhasa's eyes and beard.

him on his back on your lap and make a game of it at first, but gradually let him know you mean business. Most Lhasa Apsos are well behaved when being groomed, as they enjoy the extra attention.

In grooming the older dog, place him on his back and do his underside, chest and inner legs first. Never use a slicker brush on him, this tends to pull out and break off the coat, except on the feet. The slicker brush does a good job of fluffing up the coat around the feet and legs. Spray the dog lightly before

Most Lhasa Apsos are well behaved when being groomed, as they enjoy the one-to-one attention.

the hair around his eyes. And you have a very handsome finished product. A few minutes of playing with your dog after grooming makes it a more pleasant episode for you both.

In regard to the eyes, especially in the lighter colored Lhasa Apsos, there may be stains from eye discharge. These stains can be prevented, or at least partially prevented, by cleaning out the corners of the eyes each day, and using a stain preventative in the eye. A lack of vitamin A can cause excessive eye discharge. Cod liver oil will correct this lack very nicely.

STOOL STICKING

Your Lhasa Apso, because of his heavily feathered rear quarters, may at some time in his life have a stuck stool. Should this happen, the dog should be cleaned immediately and thoroughly as any stool left on the skin will tend to irritate it and cause a sore and/or infection. This may happen should the dog have diarrhea for any reason. The best and easiest way to prevent it is to be sure that when grooming, the coat on the tail is brushed upwards, and the coat on the hocks and legs is brushed downwards. This will eliminate any sticking because of mats in this area.

BRUSHING

A good brushing once a week should keep your Lhasa Apso in top condition. Also the brushing

The Lhasa Apso's coat is a high maintenance job. Choose the best grooming tools from your local pet shop. Photo courtesy of Wahl Clipper.

will eliminate shedding to some extent. However, the adult Lhasa Apso does not shed as one might expect with a long-coated dog. When he does drop some coat, it is usually in strands that are big enough to be easily picked up and you will not find an abundance of little hairs all over

EQUIPMENT

A good bristle brush is needed to keep dogs in top condition. A nylon brush should not be used as it has a tendency to break off the coat. A wire-type brush set in a rubber base is also of great help, especially if your dog has a heavy coat. Several steel combs

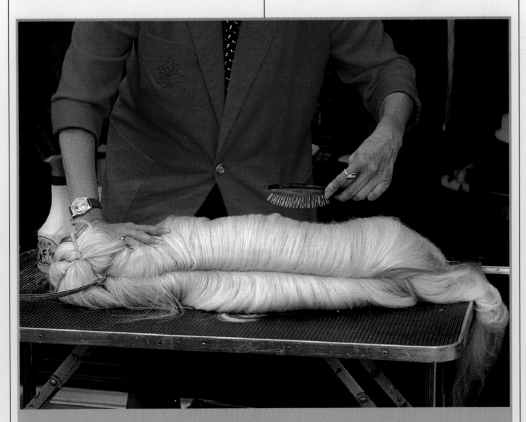

A good brushing once a week should keep your Lhasa in good condition. Part the coat down the middle of the back and brush from the skin outward.

everything. Some Apsos, usually between the ages of six to 18 months, may drop their baby coat suddenly. Or they may drop it gradually so the change over from the soft baby coat to the longer, coarser, adult coat is hardly apparent.

are needed with different sizes of teeth, from fine to coarse. All of these grooming articles can be found in your local pet shop.

FEET AND CLAWS

The bottom of the Apso's feet should be kept clean and

clipped. The hair between the toes and between the pads should be kept clipped even with the pads. If this hair is allowed to grow unchecked, it will become matted, hard, and dirty and will hurt the dog's feet. The Apso's claws should be kept clipped, and especially the dewclaws should be watched so that they don't grow too long and hurt the dog.

EARS

Special care should also be taken to keep the Apso's ears cleaned free of wax and dirt. As with any drop-eared dog, care should be taken so proper ventilation is possible. Obstructing hair should be pulled out. This can be done with the fingers or with a pair of heavy tweezers and the ears wiped clean. In bathing, care should be taken that water does not get into the dog's ears.

BATHING

There is really no set time schedule for bathing a Lhasa. Naturally before he goes into the show ring, or to an obedience trial, he should be bathed. Lhasa Apsos are naturally clean dogs. They have little or no "doggy odor." Perhaps a good rule would be to bathe a bitch after each heat is over, and bathe all Lhasas when they get dirty. They are all strictly house dogs, and do not smell, so there is certainly no need for a weekly or even monthly bath. However, during a show season, one particular dog may be bathed as much as every week for several months without any harm coming to him. One thing should be remembered, however, never rub the coat briskly with a towel, pat it gently. This will eliminate any tangles. A good practice is to let the dog shake several times, wrap him in a large towel, and blot, let him shake a few times more, wrap in a dry towel, then blot again. After this brush him dry. If you part your dog's coat while he is wet, the part will stay better. Also, a hand dryer is very helpful, even if it is merely placed several feet away from the dog, and turned on hot, it will warm the air and the dog will dry quicker and there will be less chance of his catching a cold.

In bathing the dog, use a good brand of pet shampoo. If fleas are a problem in your area, many good products are available to eliminate fleas and ticks. But use a product made especially for dogs. Most pet products will leave your dog with a pleasant smell. There are also pet rinses available to work into mats, or to make the coat more manageable. Should your dog have a particularly difficult coat, one of these might make the job of grooming easier. There are also products available for washing safely around the eyes and nose; products that will not irritate or sting the eyes. A tearless dog shampoo is acceptable for washing around the eyes also. These shampoos and parasite products are all for sale at your pet shop.

The Lhasa Apso's nails should be clipped regularly. If you are unsure how to do this, your veterinarian can show you how.

Show Lhasas kept in full coat will need to be tied up to protect their coat—never too glamorous, it's like the movie star seen in hair rollers!

SUGGESTED READING

GENERAL DOG BOOKS

The following books are all published by T.F.H. Publications, Inc. and are recommended to you for additional information:

The Atlas of Dog Breeds of the World (H-1091) by Bonnie Wilcox, DVM and Chris Walkowicz traces the history and highlights the characteristics, appearance and function of every recognized dog breed in the world. 409 different

H-1091

TS-175

breeds receive full-color treatment and individual study. Hundreds of breeds in addition to those recognized by the American Kennel Club and the Kennel Club of Great Britain are included—the dogs of the world complete! The ultimate reference work, comprehensive coverage, intelligent and delightful discussions. The perfect gift book.

Canine Lexicon (TS-175) by Andrew DePrisco and James Johnson, is an up-to-date encyclopedic dictionary for the dog person. It is the most complete single volume on the dog ever published covering more breeds than any other book as well as other relevant topics, including health, showing, training, breeding, anatomy, veterinary terms, and much more. No dog book before has ever offered this many stunning color photographs of all breeds, dog sports, and topics (over 1300 in full color).

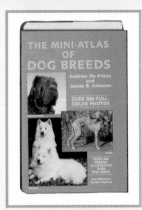

H-1106

A very successful spin-off of the *Atlas* is *The Mini-Atlas of Dog Breeds* (H-1106), written by Andrew DePrisco and James B. Johnson. This compact but comprehensive book has been praised and recommended by most national dog publications for its utility and reader-friendliness. The true field guide for dog lovers.

Teaching the family dog has never been more fun and easy! *Just Say "Good Dog"* (TS-204) is a new approach in teaching dogs to be good family dogs and good house dogs. This most original manual to canine education by Linda Goodman, author and dog teacher, addresses all the basic commands and day-to-day problems as well as the considerations and responsibilities of dog ownership. Living with a dog should be a rewarding experience, and this book will show you how. Delightful illustrations by AnnMarie Freda accompany the author's fun and anecdotal text to reinforce the importance of a positive approach to dog training. *"Just Say Good Dog"* is both very informative and authoritative, as

TS-204

the author, assisted by Marlene Trunnell, offers many years of experience and know-how.

Everybody Can Train Their Own Dog (TW-113) by Angela White is a fabulous reference guide for all dog owners. This well written, easy-to-understand book covers all training topics in alphabetical order for instant location. In addition to teaching, this book provides problem solving and problem prevention techniques that are fundamental to training. All teaching methods are based on motivation and kindness, which bring out the best of a dog's natural ability and instinct.

TW-113

PS-607

H-969

How To Show Your Own Dog (PS-607) by Virginia Tuck Nichols is an all-inclusive picture of dog shows and the problems of dog handling. Interestingly and informatively written, it shows the reader how he can double the enjoyment he gets out of placing his dog in shows and by handling the dog himself. One of the best known breeders and show personalities in the East, Mrs. Nichols is eminently qualified to write a book on shows and handling. This book covers the field step by step from early training to equipment to how to behave in the ring.

Love Me, Love My Dog (TS-212) by Keith Bing and Barry Carruthers is a unique collaboration between caring veterinarians and professional dog trainers. This is a user-friendly primer written by the experts to guide owners in choosing and obtaining a dog, training and behavior modification, feeding, grooming, health care, kenneling, and the legal aspects of dog ownership. *Love Me, Love My Dog* offers the reader everything he needs to know for a healthy happy life with his dog.

Dog Breeding for Professionals (H-969) by Dr. Herbert Richards is a straightforward discussion of how to breed dogs of various sizes and how to care for newborn puppies. The many aspects of breeding (including possible problems and practical solutions) are covered in great detail. *Warning: the explicit photos of canine sexual activities may offend some readers.*

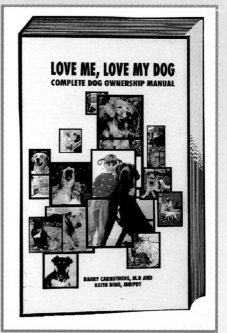

TS-212